Hubble-Bubble

by Alison Hedger

New things to do in music sessions with the very young.

Pre-School and Early Key Stage 1

TEACHER'S BOOK
Easy piano accompaniments with chord symbols. Contains songs, including two for Harvest, rhymes, actions, percussion, introduction to note values, rhythm, pitch and dynamic control.

CONTENTS

Matching Tape Cassette, Order No. GA10744.

© Copyright 1993 Golden Apple Productions
A division of Chester Music Limited
8/9 Frith Street, London W1V 5TZ

Order No. GA10736
ISBN 0-7119-3523-8

1. KANGAROO JUMPING

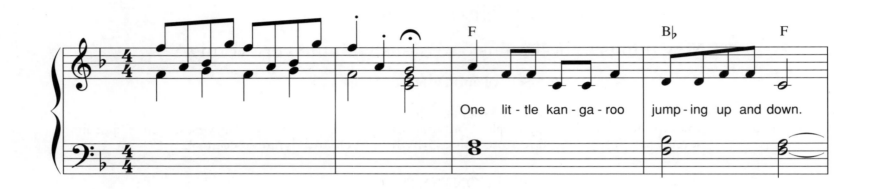

One lit - tle kan - ga - roo jump - ing up and down.

One lit - tle kan - ga - roo jump - ing all a - round. One lit - tle kan - ga - roo hav - ing lots of fun,

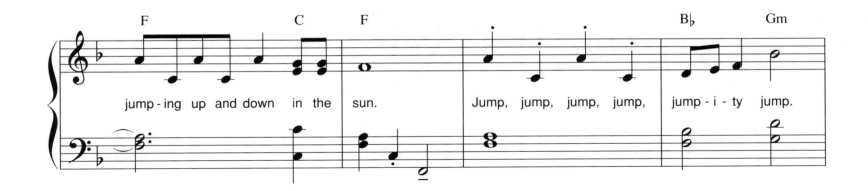

jump - ing up and down in the sun. Jump, jump, jump, jump, jump - i - ty jump.

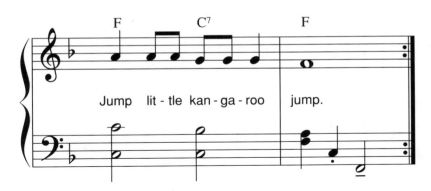

Jump lit - tle kan - ga - roo jump.

Verse two: TWO little kangaroos
Verse three: THREE little kangaroos
etc.

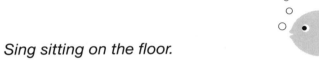

Sing sitting on the floor.

Repeat as many times as needed, counting the kangaroos on fingers.

Count the number of children taking part, and have that number of "kangaroos" literally jumping all around to a repeat of the music.

2. CLAP AND COUNT IN 2 TIME

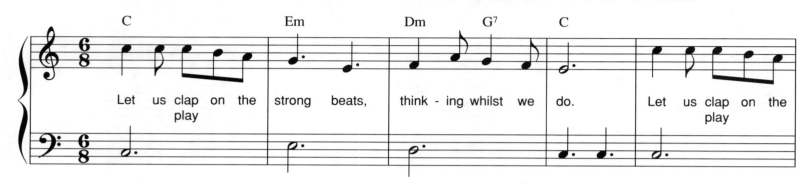

Let us clap on the
play
strong beats, think - ing whilst we do. Let us clap on the
play

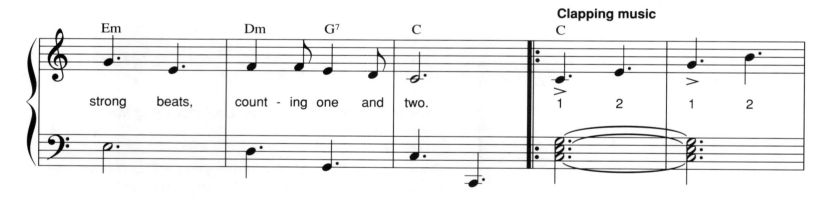

Clapping music

strong beats, count - ing one and two.

1 2 1 2

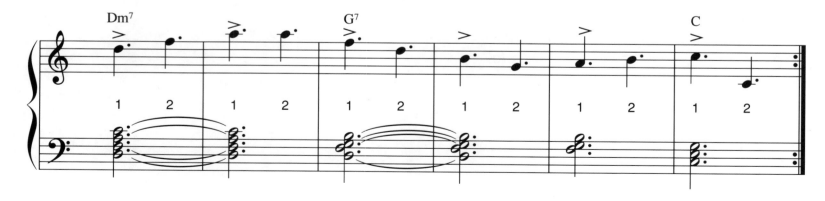

Sometimes use percussion instruments instead of clapping. These should be played softly and in time.

3. CLAP AND COUNT IN 3 TIME

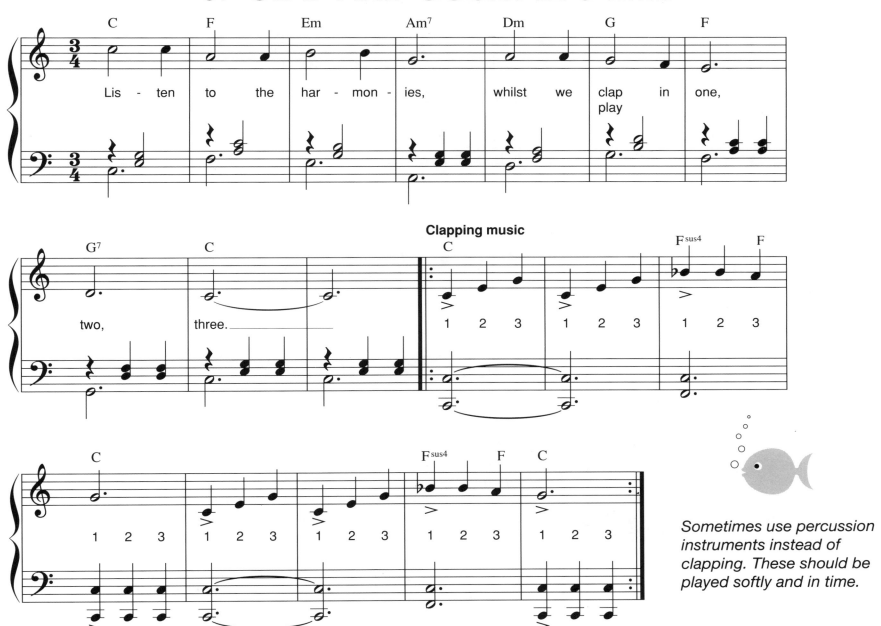

Sometimes use percussion instruments instead of clapping. These should be played softly and in time.

4. WHAT CAN WE FIND IN THE TOY BOX?

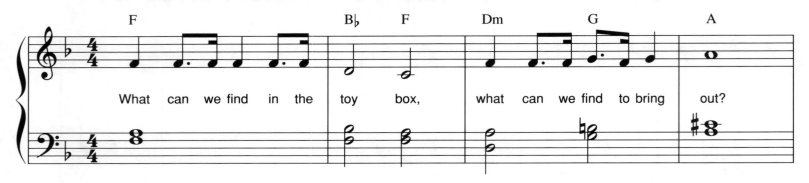

What can we find in the toy box, what can we find to bring out?

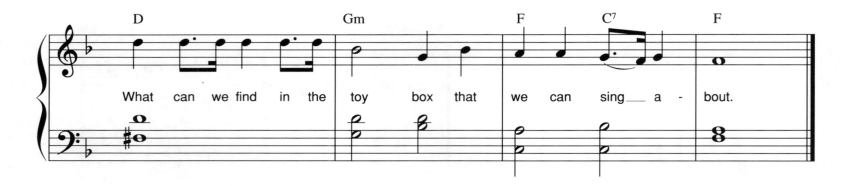

What can we find in the toy box that we can sing a - bout.

Have a large box of toys and assorted items that usually find their way into a toy box. Pull out things one by one and sing a song about them.

For example: a lamb – Mary had a little lamb
small umbrella – Rain, rain go away
train – Down at the station

The list of songs will be long once you start to think this way!

5. KNICKERTY KNACKERTY KNOO-KNOO-KNOO

Knickerty knackerty knoo-knoo-knoo,
Copy exactly what I do.

Comb your hair	(*echo*: comb your hair)
Brush your teeth	(*echo*: brush your teeth)
Blow your nose	(*echo*: blow your nose)
Wash your face	(*echo*: wash your face)
Scratch your head	(*echo*: scratch your head)
Stroke your chin	(*echo*: stroke your chin)
Lift a foot	(*echo*: lift a foot)
Bend your knees	(*echo*: bend your knees)

Plus anything else that comes to mind.

6. LIKE THIS!

All do the gold-fish swim ___ All do the gold-fish swim ___ All do the gold-fish swim ___ Like this! All do the gold-fish swim ___ All do the

All do the: BUNNY HOPS   DOLPHIN DIVE
              EAGLE FLAP   SPIDER CRAWL
              MONKEY WALK   PONY TROT

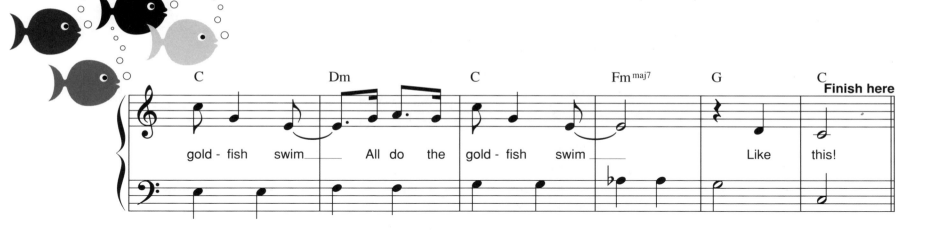

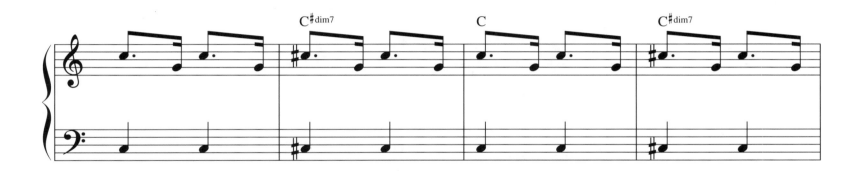

7. LITTLE PUPPY DOGS

5 lit - tle pup - py dogs play - ing in the park. 1 hurt his paw, and then there were 4
4 lit - tle pup - py dogs play - ing in the park. 1 banged his knee, and then there were 3
3 lit - tle pup - py dogs play - ing in the park. 1 stepped in glue and then there were 2
2 lit - tle pup - py dogs play - ing in the park. 1 could on - ly run and then there was 1

1 lit - tle pup - py dog play - ing in the park, wan - ted his broth - ers so he be - gan to bark.

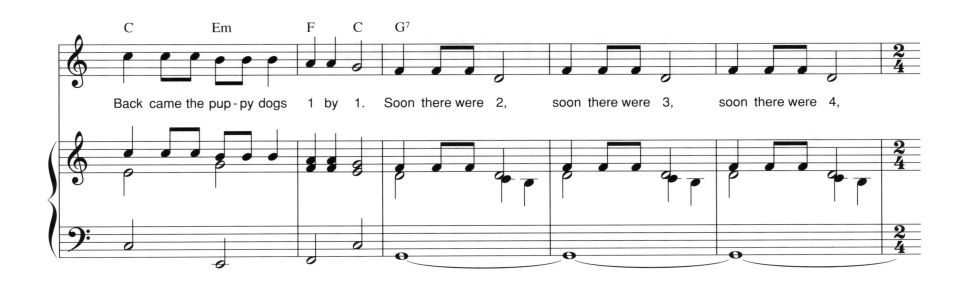

Back came the pup-py dogs 1 by 1. Soon there were 2, soon there were 3, soon there were 4,

soon there were 5 lit-tle pup-py dogs play-ing in the park. Play-ing to-geth-er un-til it was dark.

Count number of puppy dogs on fingers.

8. THE SKELETON DANCE

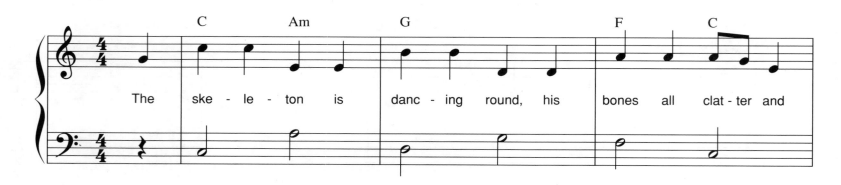

The ske - le - ton is danc - ing round, his bones all clat - ter and

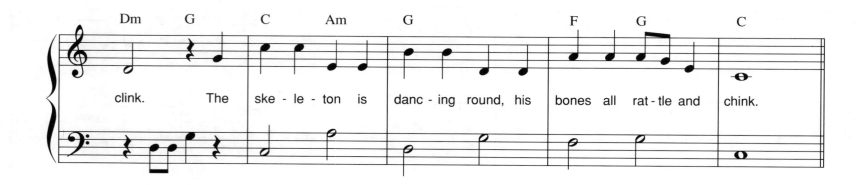

clink. The ske - le - ton is danc - ing round, his bones all rat - tle and chink.

A boney dance is called for after singing the song through.

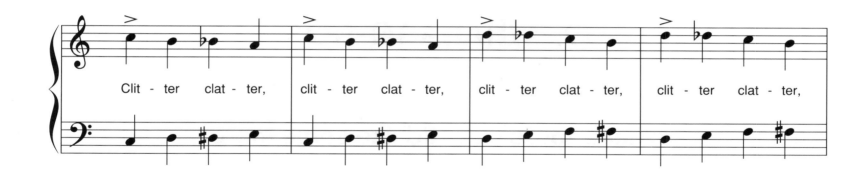

Clit - ter clat - ter, clit - ter clat - ter, clit - ter clat - ter, clit - ter clat - ter,

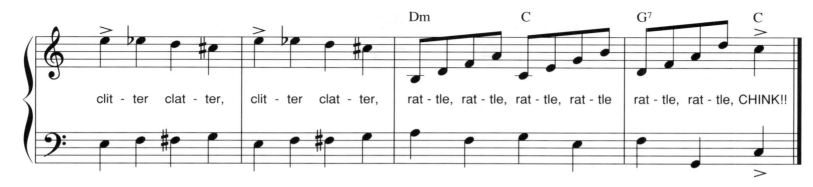

clit - ter clat - ter, clit - ter clat - ter, rat - tle, rat - tle, rat - tle, rat - tle rat - tle, rat - tle, CHINK!!

Dm *C* *G7* *C*

This section can EITHER,

be used to show controlled crescendo (getting louder) without getting faster. Children will think these two go hand in hand but they don't. It is very hard for them to keep a steady pace and get louder, in the excited expectation of the final CHINK.

OR,

use this section to show accelerando (getting faster). This time keep it ALL very quiet, but gradually quicken each CLITTER CLATTER, finishing with a flopped down pile of "bones" on a final loud, CHINK.

9. WHAT A TO-DO

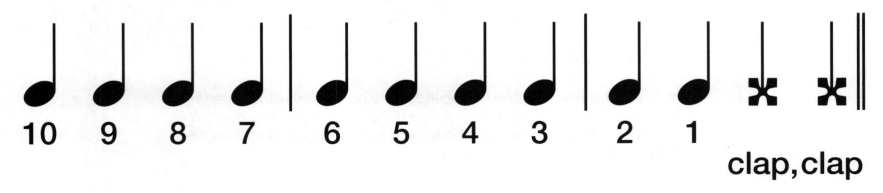

1   2   3   4

What a to-do   I'd like some more

5   6   7   8

I'm in a fix   I won't be late

9   10

Sheep in the pen

10   9   8   7   6   5   4   3   2   1

clap, clap

Children say this with their hands clasped together, releasing them to join in with the final two claps.

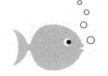

Vary the loudness of the backward counting, sometimes whispering, sometimes at medium volume, and sometimes at full strength. The two claps should reflect the dynamics used in the counting. It may be wise to finish with a whispered version.

10. THROW AND CATCH

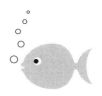

Throw and catch, throw and catch. Throw and catch in time with me.

Throw and catch, throw and catch. You can do it ea - si - ly.

Use this action song to reinforce the physical response to music.

Vary the size of the "ball" thrown. For a teeny ball, play the music quickly and up an octave.

For a medium sized "ball" play the music as normal.

For a gigantic sized "ball", the music will have to be heavy and slow.

Sometimes count 1, 2 to the music. Always make sure the "balls" are thrown and caught in time with the music.

11. JOCK MacDUFF (Crotchets)

Jock MacDuff is my best friend,
He eats with even bites all day.
He's always hungry, tummy's rumbly!
See what he can eat this way. It's......

Lettuce, broad beans, porridge, mince pies.
Cornflakes, custard, roast beef, haggis.

Jock   Mac - Duff

There are lots of other things that Jock can eat as crotchets. How about: yoghurt, biscuits, pickles, doughnuts, beetroot, bacon, sponge cake, jelly, waffles, boiled eggs, fish cakes, trifle etc.

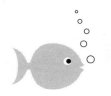

12. LITTLE WINNIE (Quavers)

Little Winnie is so skinny,
Quick to nibble, quick to feed.
She's quite an eater, none can beat her,
All is gone at double speed! It's……

Vegetable and cream-filled biscuits,
Bits of hard and smelly Cheddar.
Crumbs of cake and bits of batter.
P'raps one day she'll get much fatter!

Lit - tle   Win - nie

13. TED (Minim)

Ted likes bread, he's made that way.
He takes his time to chew, chew, chew.
He'll munch and crunch and gnaw his brunch,
Each chew will last for 2, 2, 2! It's……

Bread, toast, rolls, buns,
Chips, cake, ham, flan.

Ted

Ted can also eat the following as minims:
spam, jam, sweets and lamb.

14. COMBINING WINNIE, JOCK AND TED

Once Winnie is established as being double time to Jock, you might like to find foods that combine both their name patterns.

For example:

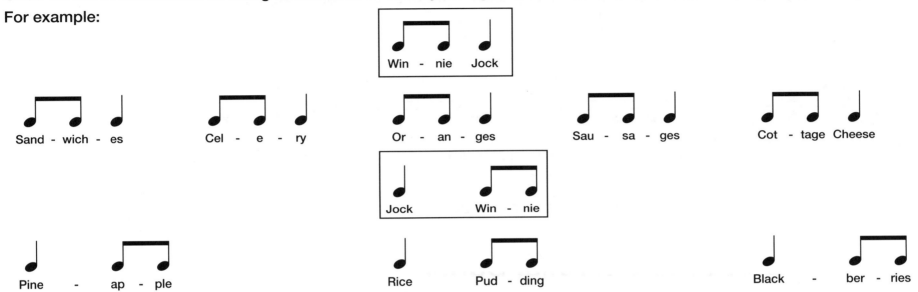

Ask the children to work out the patterns for APRICOT, FISH FINGER, APPLE PIE and LOLLIPOP.

For an impressive piece of collective speaking, have three groups of children, each with an adult leader, repeating just the foods that Winnie, Jock and Ted eat in their poem. Begin with Jock's food: steady crotchets. Next enter Winnie's list of food, at double speed of course (quavers), as the repeat of Jock's food begins. Ted's food enters last, as Winnie begins the repeat of her food. Ted's list is spoken at the slow pace of minims. All three lists of food combine. (Jock's list 3 times in all: Winnie's twice and Ted's just the once). All being well, everyone should finish together. You can hear a demonstration of the above on the matching tape. The following chart should make the format clear.

1.	Lettuce, broad beans, porridge, mince pies. Cornflakes, custard, roast beef, haggis.		
2.	Lettuce, broad beans, porridge, mince pies. Cornflakes, custard, roast beef, haggis.	Vegetables and cream-filled biscuits, Bits of hard and smelly Cheddar. Crumbs of cake and bits of batter. P'raps one day she'll get much fatter.	
3.	Lettuce, broad beans, porridge, mince pies. Cornflakes, custard, roast beef, haggis.	Vegetables and cream-filled biscuits, Bits of hard and smelly Cheddar. Crumbs of cake and bits of batter. P'raps one day she'll get much fatter.	Bread, toast, rolls, buns, Chips, cake, ham, flan!

15. CLAP, CLAP, CLAP and ROUND and ROUND

Clap, tumble forearms, stretch, bend, clap and throw arms up and out at appropriate places.

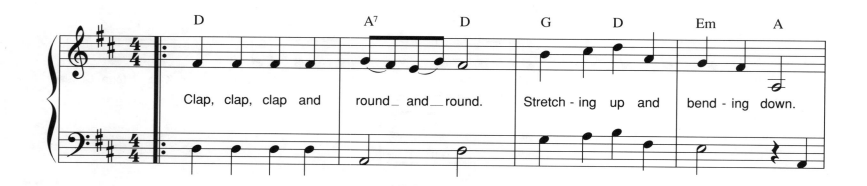

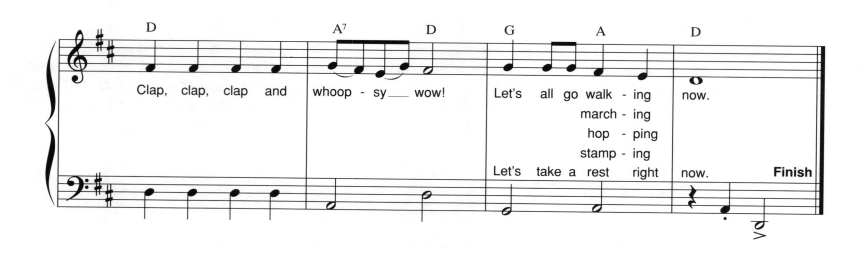

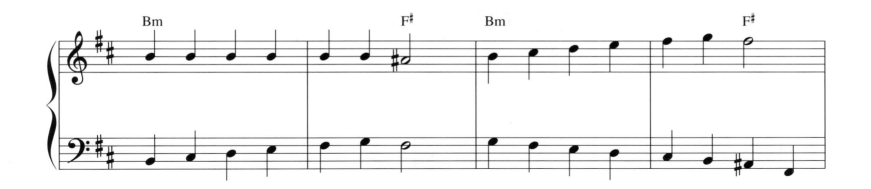

As a change, sometimes sing the song sitting and
confine the actions to the hands. Modify the words to:
Let's all do   SEWING now
                       CUTTING now
                       PAINTING now
                       WRITING now
                       COOKING now

16. OUTGROWN CLOTHES

1. Socks, socks, jol-ly old socks used to come up to my knees. But
2. Shorts, shorts, jol-ly old shorts used to come down to my knees. But
3. Shoes, shoes, jol-ly old shoes used to fit me what a treat! But

since they were bought they've be-come short and are no use to me.
now they're torn and ve-ry worn and are no use to me.
now they're holed and ve-ry old, and are no good for feet!

Use this music for the children to feel and clap the first beat of each bar. Sometimes use simple percussion instruments instead of clapping.

17. GOOD NIGHT, SLEEP TIGHT

There are several ways to use *GOOD NIGHT, SLEEP TIGHT.*

1. As a direct copy-cat exercise. You clap and say the words in the correct rhythm – the children copy exactly, waiting their turn. Vary the level of voice that you use. This too must be imitated exactly. The children both clap and say the words.

2. As an internalising exercise. The children copy you, but this time no words are spoken. The words are repeated in their heads only.

3. As 1 and 2 above, but using unpitched percussion instruments.

4. As a copy-cat exercise on pitch. The children copy not only dynamics (how loud or soft), and speed of delivery but also the note sung. Begin with one note only. Very small children are only just acquiring the skill of placing notes at the right pitch, and the majority may sound not much different from the spoken copy-cat. But with practice children will learn pitch differentiation. Make it fun by using a high pitched voice, a medium voice and a low voice, before introducing a specific note. (Use a chime bar to pitch a note if needs be.)

5. If all goes well with number 4 above, introduce 2 different notes to sing to.

6. Finally, if your children are ready, let them use chime bars to copy your sung notes. Use F and C, or G and D.

Still require the children to copy your dynamics.

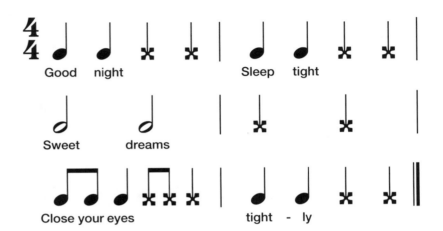

7. When pages 16–19 of this book have been covered, replace the words given with the character name

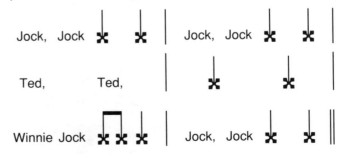

23

18. PET SHOP

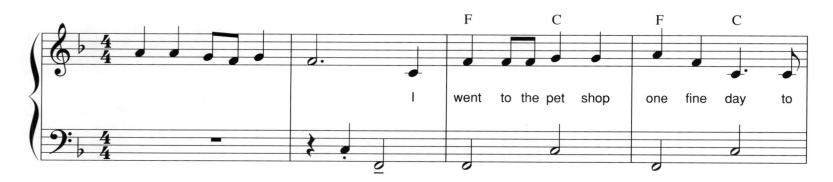

I went to the pet shop one fine day to

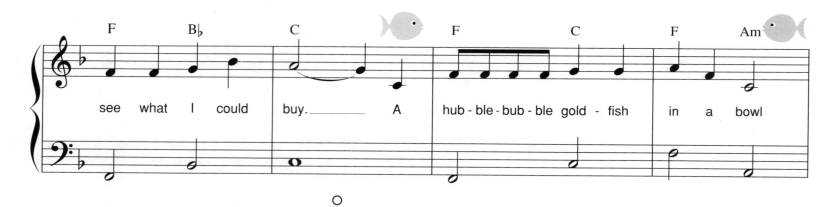

see what I could buy.___ A hub-ble-bub-ble gold-fish in a bowl

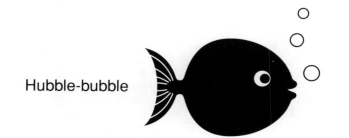

Hubble-bubble

2.   a bonny baby budgie in a cage
3.   a frisky little puppy looking fine
4.   a cuddly pretty kitten, oh, so sweet
5.   a slinky slimey long snake curled-up tight
6.   a fluffy snow-white rabbit eating greens
7.   a handsome silky hampster fast asleep

real - ly caught_ my eye. A hub - ble - bub - ble gold - fish in a bowl was

sold to me then and there._ That hub - ble - bub - ble gold - fish now is mine.

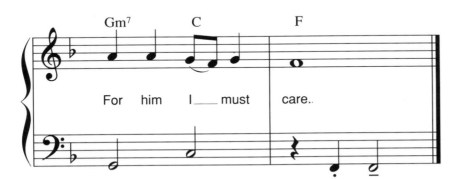

For him I_ must care..

If you wish, an extra verse can be added by repeating the music marked

 to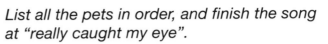

List all the pets in order, and finish the song at "really caught my eye".

19. MY WALL

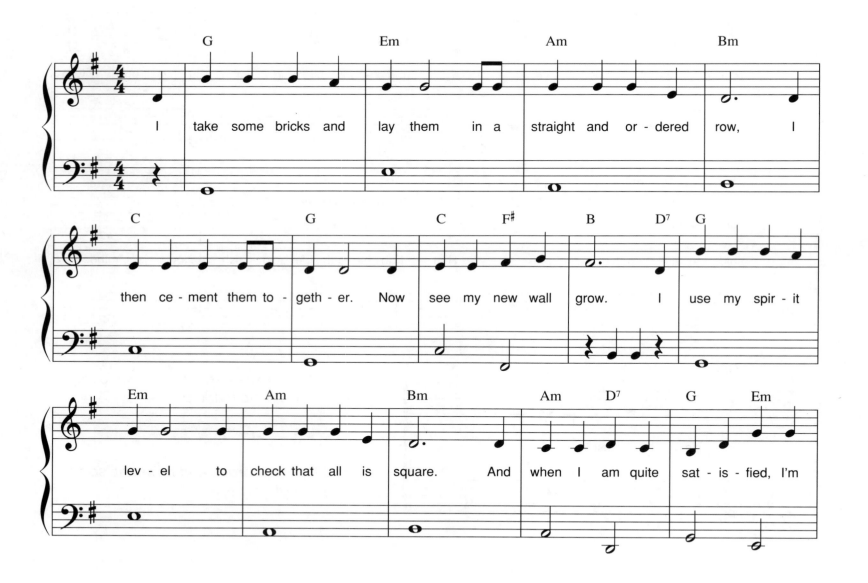

I take some bricks and lay them in a straight and or-dered row, I then ce-ment them to-geth-er. Now see my new wall grow. I use my spir-it lev-el to check that all is square. And when I am quite sat-is-fied, I'm

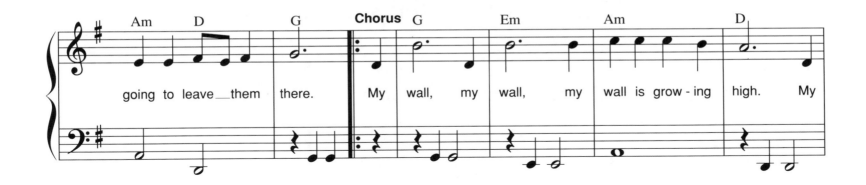

going to leave___them there. My wall, my wall, my wall is grow - ing high. My

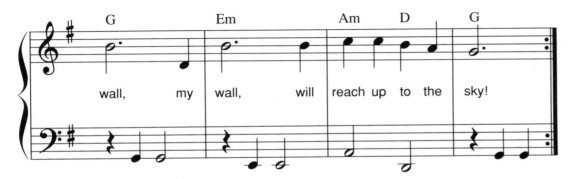

wall, my wall, will reach up to the sky!

When the song is known to the children ask them to clap along with the words.
This is quite a difficult task for the very young.
Practise clapping with the spoken words and pay particular attention to:

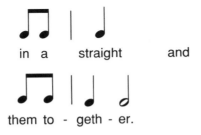

in a straight and

them to - geth - er.

Repeat each of the above several times.

20. HARVEST OF LIFE (Little Seeds)

The lit - tle seeds they fall up - on the good rich soil, and then they put down roots and then they grow up tall. We all are like those seeds, we grow up ev' - ry day. Ev' - ry day can be a day of

Arm actions can be done at "put down roots and then they grow up tall."
Add tambourines and untuned percussion as desired.

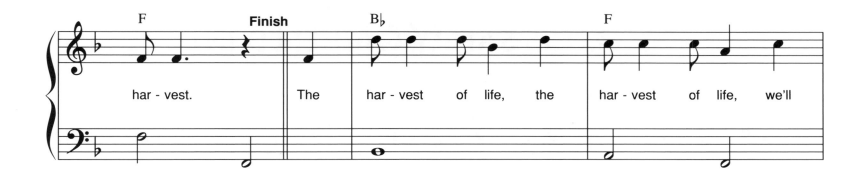

har - vest. The har - vest of life, the har - vest of life, we'll

har - vest the things we do ev' - ry day. The har - vest of life, the

har - vest of life. We'll do our ve - ry best in work and play. The lit - tle

21. ALL IS SAFELY GATHERED IN

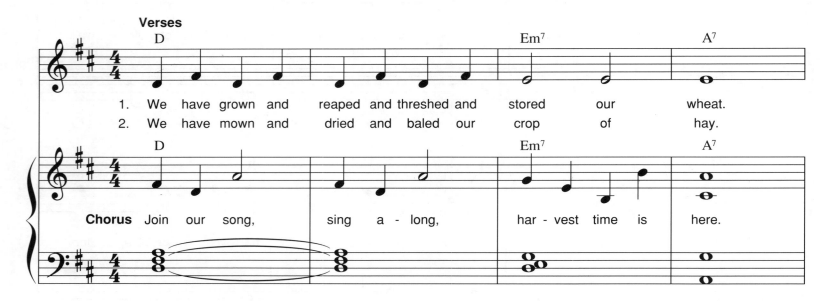

1. We have grown and reaped and threshed and stored our wheat.
2. We have mown and dried and baled our crop of hay.

Chorus Join our song, sing a - long, har - vest time is here.

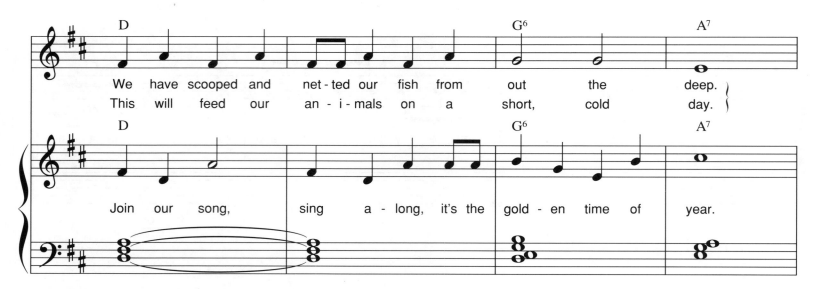

We have scooped and net - ted our fish from out the deep.
This will feed our an - i - mals on a short, the cold day.

Join our song, sing a - long, it's the gold - en time of year.

The L.H. piano part is for both the chorus and verse melody lines.

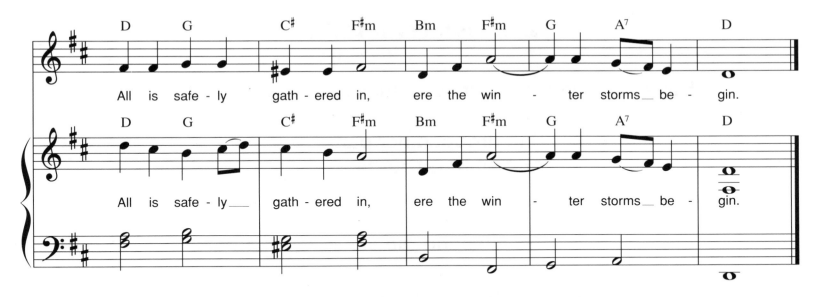

This song can be sung in unison (all sing the same tune at the same time) or the
children can be divided into two groups. If there are older children available, this will
work well at a special Harvest Assembly. The chorus is sung by everyone. The verses
are taken by the second group (older children if possible). The verses and chorus are
sung together in 2-part singing. The youngest children keep to the chorus only. The
second group also join in the first and last choruses.

Chorus	(ALL)
Verse 1	(Group 2)
Chorus + verse 1 repeated	(Groups 1 and 2)
Verse 2	(Group 2)
Chorus + verse 2 repeated	(Groups 1 and 2)
Chorus	(ALL)

This is ambitious but well worth attempting.

22. AUNTY LOLL

Have you heard of Aunty Loll, married to an ancient troll?

She dropped her pan
And whizzed her fan,

She washed her frock
Then wound the clock.

She boiled the kettle
Then struck some metal,

She slammed the door
And scrubbed the floor.

She stamped her foot
And sneezed – kerhoooooot!

She banged and bonged and crashed all day.
Aunty Loll is made that way!

 *Add appropriate sound effects to the poem.*

Printed and bound in Great Britain by
Caligraving Limited Thetford Norfolk

8/01 (40848)